# Summary

    I. Friendship             Amicizia
    II. Love                    Amore
    III. Money                Denaro
    IV. Food                  Il Mangiare
    V. Luck                   Fortuna
    VI. Trust                  Fiducia
    VII. Disappointment    Delusione
    VIII. Hope                Speranza
    IX. Family               Famiglia
    X. Hate                   Ira
    XI. Envy                  Invidia
    XII. Legality             Legalità
    XIII. Freedom           Libertà
    XIV. Ill will               Malavoglia
    XV. Risk                  Rischio
    XVI. Health               Salute
    XVII. Society              Società
    XVIII. Time and weather    Tempo
    XIX. Work and Art     Lavoro, Arte
    XX. Latin Proverbs – A Must

# Introduction

*Proverbs say a lot of things on people; describe their habits, their joys and fears.*

*They are not made to impress tourists or foreign countries. Almost confidential, they are made by the people to criticize themselves and educate their children with morals.*

*Reading this book if you love Italy is a way to come closer to its culture with a folkloric scent and to learn more about this beautiful country.*

*If you speak Italian and wish to improve your language level and to find a proverb to say in every situation, this book might also be a helpful friend.*

**"La Ciliegina sulla Torta"** *includes 20 chapters and more than 400 proverbs with their literal translations and explanations on how to use them. The last chapter goes through Latin proverbs, a must in Italy's top society!*

*Have a nice trip!*

# 1. Friendship — Amicizia

**Gli amici si riconoscono nel bisogno.**

*We recognize friends in need.*

Going through tribulations and hard times, the friends that remain and assist are sincere.

**Meglio un aiuto che cento consigli.**

*Better a help than a hundred tips.*

**Amicizia e maccheroni, se non son caldi, non son buoni.**

Friendship and macaronis, if they are not hot, they are not good.

**Né amici riconciliati, né cavoli ricucinati.**

Neither friends that made up, nor cabbages warmed up a second time.

*Friends that made up after arguing will not be the same as before. It is therefore no good!*

**Amicizia rinnovata e minestra riscaldata non valgon niente.**

*A renewed friendship and a soup warmed up a second time are worth nothing.*


**Vecchia amicizia presto rinverdisce.**

*An old friendship quickly becomes green again.*

*If something causes friends not to see one another for a while, the two mates will quickly remember good habits when they see each other again.*


**Amicizia di viaggio poco dura.**

*A friendship made traveling, lasts little time.*

*A friendship made during a trip or a party will not have strong bases to last for a long time.*

*Close to this proverb:*


**Amico di bicchiere dura quanto un fuoco di paglia.**

*"Glass friend" lasts as long as a hay fire.*

*By "glass friend" understand a friend made during a party, or someone you had a drink with.*

*By "hay fire" understand something quick, flash in the pan.*


**Prendere e non dare, l'amicizia non può durare.**

*Taking without giving back, friendship will not last.*

*Generosity always has to be given back.*


**L'amicizia si cerca col moccolo e l'odio si trova senza lanterna.**

*Friendship is searched with the tip of a candle, whereas hatred is found with no lamp.*

*A real friend is hard to find.*


**Finché la pentola bolle, l'amicizia canta.**

*Friendship sings as long as the pan boils.*

*In prosperity, friends are abundant and the house is full of people, when tribulations occur, the house will empty itself out.*
*This expression is close to:*


**La porta dice:-Porta!**

*The door says: Bring (something)!*

**Il vero amico entra quando tutti sono usciti.**

*The real friend comes in when all have gone out.*

**Gli amici si conoscono nei bisogni**

*The friends are found in trouble.*

**Gli amici certi si vedono nelle cose incerte.**

*The true friends can be seen in unsure situations.*

**Finito il guadagno, finito l'amicizia.**

*When the gains (earnings) are gone, friendship is finished.*

*Le amicizie si fanno in prigione.*

Friendship is made in jail.

Real friends are found during hard times and tribulations.

*Chi trova un amico trova un tesoro.*

Who finds a friend, finds a treasure.

*Gli amici non son mai troppi.*

Friends are never too many.

*Fatti amici in tempo di pace che ti servano in tempo di guerra.*

Make friends during times of peace that will be useful to you during war times.

*Chi ama l'amico,*
*L'onora in presenza,*
*Lo loda in assenza,*
*L'aiuta in necessità.*

Who loves a friend

*Will honor him in his presence,*
*Will praise him in his absence*
*And will help him when he is in need.*

**L'amico è come il vino : se è buono migliora col tempo.**

*Friends are like wine: if they are good, they will get better with time.*

**Amico di tutti, amico di nessuno.**

*Everybody's friend, nobody's friend.*

*Of course one can know many people, but real friends are scarce. Therefore someone saying he or she is everyone's friend is mistaken on the meaning of friendship and therefore is no one's friend.*

# 11. Love — Amore

**L'allegria fa campare, la passione fa crepare.**

Happiness makes one live, passion makes one die.

**Amante non sia, chi coraggio non ha.**

Lover will not be the one who has no courage.

**Solo l'audace ha fortuna in amore.**

Only the daring is lucky in love.

**Uomo pauroso non bacia donna bella.**

Worrisome man does not kiss beautiful woman.

**Chi ama teme.**

Who loves also fears.

Someone will always worry for one's other half.

***Chi ama brucia.***

*Who loves also burns.*

*In the way that he or she will suffer from doubts and passion.*


***Chi ama non vede.***

*The one who loves does not see.*

*Love is blind.*


***Quanto più si ama, meno si conosce.***

*The more one loves, the less one knows.*

*Love brings a false image of the person.
Love is blind.*


***Chi ama me, ama il mio cane.***

*Who loves me, will also love my dog.*

*Love is everything and includes every aspect of someone's personality, therefore the person's faults, of course, but also the person's dog...and much more...*

*Ama chi ti ama e chi non ti ama lascia, chi t'ama di buon cuore stringi ed abbraccia.*

Love who loves you, and who does not love you, let go, and who loves you with an open heart, give a big hug and hold tight.

*Amare e non essere amato è tempo perso.*

To love and not to be loved back is a waste of time.

*Chi ama ha le tasche piene di speranza.*

Who loves has the pockets full of hope.

*Ama come se un giorno tu dovessi odiare e Odia come se un giorno tu dovessi amare.*

Love just like if one day you were to hate, and Hate just like if one day you were to love.

*Amami poco ma amami sempre.*
Love me little but always.

***Chi ama tutti non ama nessuno.***

*Who loves everyone, does not love anybody.*

***Dell'amore non si può fare a metà.***

*One cannot love half way.*

*Feelings cannot be divided, true love cannot be measured.*

***Uomo ammogliato, uccello in gabbia.***

*Married man, bird in a cage.*

***D'amore sono morti pochi.***

*Not many died from love.*

***L'amore è bello per chi lo impara.***

*Love is beautiful for the one learning it.*

*Once you really know your other half, a lot of the charm has faded away.*

**L'amore è come un fiore: se non s'annaffia muore.**

*Love is like a flower: if you don't water it, it will die.*

**Amore con amore si paga.**

*Love is paid with love.*

**Dove è amore è gelosia.**

*Where love is, jealousy is too.*

# III. Money      Denaro

**Il bene non è mai troppo**

*Good is never too much.*

**Il denaro apre tutte le porte.**

*Money opens every door.*

**Nessuno ha mai abbastanza.**

*Someone never has enough.*

*Someone always hopes to have more than the present conditions.*

**L'abbondanza fa arroganza.**

*Abundance makes arrogance.*

**L'abbondanza rende vile ogni cosa gentile.**

*Abundance makes every kind thing evil.*

*Someone loses the simple joys of existence with too much money and fails to be happy.*

**Dopo l'abbondaza viene la carestia.**

After abundance, insolvency.

**L'acqua va dov'è l'acqua.**

Water goes where water is.

Water gathers in a basin in the wild. In society, money always goes back to rich and powerful families.

**Acquisto risparmiato, denaro guadagnato.**

Saved purchase, earned money.

What one does not spend automatically remains as savings.

**Acquisto caro, buon risparmio.**

Expensive purchase, good saving.

*Expensive products are often of a better quality than the cheapest ones, therefore in the long term, it could be considered as a saving and give a longer use to the person, allowing him or her to save money.*

**Con le ali d'oro si vola molto in alto.**

*With golden wings, one flies further.*

*Money opens many doors and gives more possibilities.*

**Quando il portafoglio è grosso**
**Tutti gli amici ti saltano addosso;**
**Quando resta pulito**
**Addio compagno e arrivederci amico.**

*When the wallet is fat*
*Friends jump on you,*
*When you stay clean,*
*So long mates and good bye friends.*

*Friendship is too often interested, when the false acquaintances realize that there is no more money to benefit from, they take distance.*

**Il fuoco dell'amore non fa bollire le pentole.**

The fire of love does not make the pan boil.

**L'argento tondo compra tutto il mondo.**

Round money (understand "coins") can buy the whole world.

**Quando il povero arricchisce, diventa un tiranno.**

When a poor gets rich, he becomes a tyrant.

**Chi è povero dorme tranquillo.**

Who is poor can sleep quietly.

Poor people are said not to have anxieties or problems on how to manage money!

**Chi non ne ha non ne perde.**

Who does not have, does not lose.

***Chi ha la casa vuota lascia la porta aperta.***

Who has an empty house, leaves the door open.

***Chi è povero ognun lo fugge.***

Everyone flees the poor.

***Caduto in povertà, persi gli amici.***

Fallen in poverty, friends are all lost.

***La povertà è come la morte, invocata da molti e fuggita da tutti.***

Poverty is like death, invoked by all and fled from all.

***Il denaro è il re del mondo.***

Money is the King of the world.

***Il denaro non ha odore.***

Money has no smell.

***Il denaro è il nerbo della guerra.***

*Money if the sinews of war.*

***Il denaro non ama la prigione.***

*Money doesn't like to be in jail.*

*Money will try to be spent, and flee from one wallet to another; therefore it will not like to be enclosed in a safe.*

***Nel palazzo della giustizia prima passa il denaro e poi la legge.***

*In a court house, first come the money and then the law.*

***Il denaro fa l'uomo avaro.***

*Money makes the stingy man.*

*The need to have always more money will make the rich man extremely economical.*

# IV. Food   Il Mangiare

**L'appetito vien mangiando.**

Appetite comes as you eat.

**Aver l'acquolina in bocca.**

To make one's mouth water.

When we think of all the exquisite specialties we can eat in Italy, this expression is often used, and thank goodness!

**Meglio la notte del trattore che quella del dottore.**

Better the caterer's night than the doctor's.

Better eat than be sick.

**Ogni aceto fu vino.**

Every vinegar has been wine.

*Before being sad and evil, one was perhaps outgoing and enthusiastic and before being corrupted, one was perhaps kind and honest.*

**Ogni aiuto è buono, tranne quello a tavola.**

*All the help is good to take, except at the table.*

*A help to eat something is a piece of cake less to savor!*

**Quel che si mangia con appetito non si racconta al medico.**

*One doesn't say to the doctor what one ate with appetite.*

**Prima si mangia e poi si ragiona.**

*First, we eat, and then we think.*

*No good decision can be taken with an empty stomach.*

**Chi ha mangiato non pensa a chi ha fame.**

*Who has eaten does not think of who is hungry.*

***Quando uno ha mangiato, si chiede a cosa serva la cucina.***

*Who has eaten wonders what the cook is useful for.*

***Chi mangia piano vive sano.***

*Someone who eats slowly, lives healthy.*

***Mangia come un bue e bevi come un asino.***

*Eat like a cow and drink like a donkey.*

*Cows eat chewing for a long time and donkeys always drink calmly and in little quantity.*

***Il mangiare insegna a bere.***

*Eating teaches to drink.*

*The quality of the meal determines the wine to drink, never the other way round.*

***Non mangiar crudo e non andar a piede ignudo.***

*Don't eat raw and don't walk bare foot.*

*Someone eating raw products risks to have food poisoning and someone walking without shoes can get hurt under the foot.*
*You might of course chose to ignore this old tale, but you will not be able to say that no one told you about it!*


**Chi mangia e non beve è sazio e non lo crede.**

*Who eats and doesn't drink is fed but doesn't know it.*


**Si deve mangiare per vivere e non vivere per mangiare.**

*Eat to live and don't live to eat.*


**Mangia e lascia mangiare.**

*Eat and allow (the others) to eat.*

*This proverb is often used to describe someone earning money in a disrespectful way and still oppressing the ones around him, depending of this little money to feed themselves.*

***Vivi e lascia vivere***

Live and allow (the others) to live.

***Chi troppo mangia, mangia per poco.***

Who eats too much will not eat for long.

Over-indulgence at meals will cause sickness.

***Se ti preme sanità, non mangiare a sazietà.***

If you want to be healthy, don't eat too much.

***Con pasti succulenti si scava la fossa con i propri denti.***

With exquisite dishes, you dig your grave with your teeth.

***Chi troppo mangia male invecchia.***

Who eats too much, will not grow old well.

***Bisogna mangiare da sano e bere da malato.***

*You have to eat like a healthy person and drink like a sick one.*

**L'animale divora, l'uomo mangia, il gentiluomo assapora.**

*The animal devours, the man eats and the gentleman savors.*

**Chi comincia a mangiare comincia la guerra.**

*Who starts to eat starts the war. From birth, everybody has to make his place and fight for survival.*

# V. Luck      Fortuna

**Non tutti i mali vengono per nuocere.**

*All the suffering does not necessarily come to harm.*

*What does not kill you makes you stronger.*

**Trovare la strada fatta.**

*Find one's way already made.*

**La fortuna va presa per i capelli.**

*Fortune has to be seized by the hair.*

*Seize the opportunity while you still can.*

**Il pesce si prende quando passa.**

*The fish has to be caught as its swims by.*

***La fortuna non fa anticamera.***

*Luck does not stay in the waiting-room.*

***Non dire mai alla fortuna : Aspetta.***

*Never say to luck: Wait!*

***Ogni lasciato, è perso.***

*Something left out is lost.*

***La fortuna non ha casa.***

*Luck does not have a home.*

*Fortune can knock on every door. Both rich and poor families can be lucky.*

***La fortuna balla un po' con tutti.***

*Luck dances a little bit with everyone.*

***La fortuna se ti vuole ti cerca.***

*If luck wants you, luck finds you.*

***La fortuna ha i piedi di vetro.***

*Luck has glass feet.*

*It can also quickly break and fade away.*

***Fortuna e vento son le mani del Signore.***

*Luck and wind are in the hands of the Lord.*

*God is said to order the winds and the good opportunities.*

***La fortuna è la dote dei pazzi.***

*Luck is the crazy men's joker.*

***Dopo la fortuna viene la sfortuna.***

*After fortune comes misfortune.*

*The cycles are said to last seven years. After glory comes despair.*

***Chi sta sulla fortuna sta sulle sabbie mobili.***

*The one, who stands on good fortune, stands on moving sands.*

**Ogni sette anni la fortuna gira.**

*Fortune turns every seven years.*

**La fortuna aiuta chi la tenta.**

*Luck helps the one who goes for it.*

**La fortuna va col coraggio.**

*Luck goes with courage.*

**Contro la fortuna non c'è forza alcuna.**

*Against (bad) luck, no strength will do.*

*When a nice project, even inventive and resourceful, is not accompanied by luck, everything will fail.*

**Chi nasce fortunato è sempre fortunato.**

*The one born lucky will always be lucky.*

***Si corre più con la fortuna che con i cavalli.***

*One runs more with luck than with horses.*

*Fortune and good luck can climb the highest mountains and is faster than every other means.*


***Alla fortuna bisogna sempre lasciare aperta una finestra.***

*One should always keep a window open to good fortune.*

# VI. Trust      Fiducia

**hi t'accarezza più di quel che suole o t'ha ingannato o ingannato ti vuole.**

*Someone caressing you more than he should is either using you or wants to use you.*

**Chi ti adula ti tradisce.**

*Someone who adulates you will betray you.*

*Someone's enthusiasm could hide interest and fallacy.*

**Chi ti loda in presenza ti biasima in assenza.**

*The one who praises you in your presence will disown you in your absence.*

**A tre cose non credere: ad alchimista povero, a medico malato e a eremita grasso.**

*Don't believe three things: a poor chemist, a sick doctor and a fat hermit.*

**Conoscenti molti e amici pochi.**

*Many acquaintances and little friends.*

**Parla all'amico come se dovesse diventar nemico.**

*Talk to a friend just as if he was to become your enemy.*

**Se vuoi un amico dagli un fiasco di vino,
Se vuoi un nemico digli la verità.**

*If you want a friend, give him a wine jug,
If you want an enemy, tell him the truth.*

**Amor vuol fede e l'asino, il bastone.**

*Love wants trust, whereas a donkey wants a stick.*

**La sfiducia è la madre della sicurezza.**

*The mistrust is mother of safety.*

***Chi troppo si fida spesso grida.***

*Who trusts too much, often cries.*

***Chi più si fida più è ingannato.***

*The one who trusts the most is the most fooled.*

***Chi disse fidati, disse bene,***
***Chi disse non ti fidare, disse meglio.***

*The one who says "trust", says well.*
*The one who says "watch out", says better.*

***Di chi non si fida non ti fidare.***

*Don't trust the one not trusting anyone.*

***Fiducia delusa non tollera scusa.***

*Deceived trust doesn't tolerate excuses.*

***Abbi molta fede e poca fiducia.***

*Have a lot of Faith and little trust.*

***Chi fiducia non ha, fiducia non trova.***

*The one, who does not trust anyone, will not find other people's trust.*

***Abbi fiducia ma chiudi la porta.***

*Trust but lock your door.*
*Trust has limits, always keep your safety in mind.*

***Dall'esperienza nasce il sospetto.***

*Experience gives birth to suspicion.*

***E' bene sospettare anche del padre.***

*It is good to suspect also your father.*

***Chi è in difetto, è in sospetto.***

*Who is in fault will suspect.*

***Il sospetto canta la mattina con gli angeli e cena la sera col diavolo.***

*Suspicion sings in the morning with angels and dines in the evening with the devil. Doubts produce a vicious circle causing always deeper anxieties and fears.*

# VII. Disappointment
## Delusione

**Chi troppo abbraccia nulla stringe.**

Who hugs too much never embraces.

Who always tries to have higher objectives ends up with nothing, not even past victories as they faded away.


**L'abito non fa il monaco.**

Clothes don't make the monk.

Never judge a book by its cover.


**Il velo non fa la monaca.**

The veil does not make the nun.


**La libreria non fa l'uomo dotto.**
The book-shelf does not make the wise man (erudite).

***La barba non fa il filosofo.***

*The beard does not make the philosopher.*

***La croce non fa il cavaliere.***

*The cross does not make the knight.*

***Adamo per una mela perse l'orto.***

*Adam lost the garden for an apple.*

***I falsi amici ballano con le lepri e cacciano con i cani.***

*The false friends dance with the hares and hunt with the dogs.*

***Amore fa amore e crudeltà fa sdegno.***

*Love generates love whereas cruelty makes disdain.*

***Non c'è rosa senza spine.***

*No rose without thorns.*

*There is always a drawback to everything.*

**La rosa vive tra le spine.**

*The rose lives within the thorns.*

**Perdere fa sangue cattivo.**

*Losing makes bad blood.*

*The bitterness one feels after a failure is so that one may become grave and tensed. This can damage one's health in the long term.*

**Perdere fa parte del gioco.**

*Losing is part of the game.*

**Chi gioca per ridere perde sul serio.**

*Someone playing to laugh is losing seriously.*

**Chi perde ha sempre torto.**

*The one who loses is always wrong.*

***Guai ai vinti!***

Calamity to the losers!

Not only is it difficult to fail, but the losers have to face the disdain of those who took their place.

***Non si può sempre vincere.***

One cannot always win.

***Vince molto chi non gioca.***

The one who does not play (understand gamble), earns a lot.

This is for money games and gambling, the one who chooses not to gamble will save money!

***Chi soffre impara.***

The one, who suffers, learns.

Experience is the sum of all the failures.

To learn the hard way.

***Godi fin che puoi che il soffrir non manca mai.***

*Make the most of every moment, suffering never lacks.*

***A chi Dio vuol bene manda tribolazioni.***

*God sends tribulations to the ones He likes.*

# VIII. Hope — Speranza

**Passasse l'angelo e dicesse Amen.**

*When the angel passed by, he said Amen.*

*This expression is said in Rome for an impossible wish. When an angel passes by and says Amen, the wish will come true. Therefore when someone sees a very beautiful woman or a nice car, he repeats this expression to make a wish.*

**Le tribolazioni sono la scala del Cielo.**

*Tribulations make the ladder to Heaven.*

**Finché si vive si spera.**

*As long as one lives, one hopes.*

**La speranza è l'ultima a morire.**

*Hope is the last one to die.*

*I cavalli della speranza volano, ma gli asini vanno al passo.*

The horses of hope fly, whereas the donkeys walk.

*Chi ha cammina e chi spera vola.*

Who has, walks and who hopes, flies.

*Nel paese della speranza non s'ingrassa.*

In the country of Hope, one does not gain weight.

Even though dreams feed the mind, they do not generate income.

*La speranza è il sogno dell'uomo desto.*

Hope is the dream of the awoken man.

Hope exists also for someone down to earth and rational.

*La speranza è il rimedio della disperazione.*

Hope is the remedy of despair.

*Senza speranza non si semina.*

One does not sow without hope.

*Fede, occhio e onore non soffrono offesa.*

Faith, eye and honor cannot stand offence.

The eye is very fragile and will not bear the slightest hit without being injured. The honor and the faith are the same, in a more subjective way of course.

*Con la Fede si spostano le montagne.*

With faith, one can move mountains.

*Alla fede tutto è possibile.*

With faith, everything is possible.

*Con la fede e l'amore non si scherza.*

No one should joke with faith and love.

*Fa male chi crede troppo e chi crede poco.*

*The one who believes too much suffers, just as the one who does not believe.*

*One should not be blinded by dreams but should have hope.*

**A qualcuno bisogna credere.**

*Everyone needs to believe.*

**Chi non crede non è creduto.**

*Who doesn't believe is not believed.*

**Quel che si vuole presto si crede.**

*One believes what one desires.*

**Si crede più al male che al bene.**

*One believes more easily evil than good.*

**Chi ama crede.**

*Who loves, believes.*
*One trusts the people one loves.*

***Se ti danno fiducia, prendila ma non la restituire.***

*If someone gives you trust, take it but don't give it back.*

*It could be a trap to trust someone too kind.*

# IX. Family — Famiglia

**La Mamma è l'angelo della famiglia.**

*The Mum is the Family's angel.*

**Aiuta i tuoi e gli altri se puoi.**

*Help yourself and (help) the others if you can.*

**Le anime belle s'incontrano.**

*The beautiful souls get to meet one another.*

**Beata la famiglia dove prima nasce la figlia.**

*Blessed is the family where first is born a daughter.*

**Capo di famiglia, capo di pensieri.**

*Family master, master of thought.*

***Il padre di famiglia deve avere quattro occhi e dieci mani.***

*The father of a family should have four eyes and ten hands.*

*The father should maintain the family financially and must also pay attention to his loved ones.*

***Chi vuole stare in pace in famiglia deve essere cieco, sordo, muto e star poco a casa.***

*Someone wishing to be in peace in family must be blind, deaf and dumb, and should not be home often!*

***Una mamma fa per cento figli e cento figli non fanno per una mamma.***

*A mother does for a hundred sons what a hundred sons don't do for a mother.*

*A mum will always do her best to provide everything to her family. When she is aging, many children will not be able to do the same for her.*

***Un padre campa cento figli e cento figli non campano un padre.***

*A father makes a hundred sons live, whereas a hundred sons don't make a father live.*

**Se muore il gallo, la chioccia raccoglie i pulcini,
Se muore la chioccia, i pulcini si disperdono.**

*If the rooster dies, the hen collects the chicks.
If the hen dies, the chicks disperse.*

**Padre e padrone, anche se han torto, han sempre ragione.**

*Father and boss, even if they are wrong, they are always right.*

**Meglio pianga il ragazzo che il padre.**

*Better that the son cries than the father.*

*Even if a child has to learn the hard way, this suffering is necessary for his or her future... If the parents fail to make the child understand, he or she might make mistakes that will cause a terrible sorrow to the parents.*

**L'arte del padre è mezza imparata.**

The father's art (understand profession) is half way learnt.

The children get to naturally familiarize themselves with their parents' profession watching them.


**Chi vuol saper della figlia guardi la madre.**

Who wants to know about the daughter must look at the mother.

Mothers and daughters often look alike.


**Figlio senza dolore, madre senza amore.**

Son with no pain, mother with no love.

The education has to be harsh sometimes for the children's sake.


**Se la madre scivola, la figlia cade.**

If the mother slips, the daughter falls.

If the mother makes a mistake, the daughter will do worse.

***Vede più una madre con un occhio che un padre con una dozina.***

*A mother sees more with one eye than the father with a dozen.*

***La madre sa per prima e il padre per ultimo.***

*The mother is the first to know and the father the last one.*

***La madre è sempre certa, il padre mai.***

*The mother is always sure and the father never.*

*In term of family links of course as well as secrets and little stories.*

***L'amore della madre non invecchia.***

*The love of a mother does not age.*

*Nothing tarnishes the love of a mother.*

***Tre figli e una madre, quattro diavoli per un padre.***

*Three children and a mother, four devils for a father.*

# X. Hate     Ira

**Brutto è il cane che non abbaia.**

*Evil is the dog that does not bark.*

**Can che vuol mordere non abbaia.**

*The dog that wants to bite does not bark.*

**Dal vino dolce si fa aceto forte.**

*With sweet wine, we make strong vinegar.*

**Chi mal ti vuole mala ambiasciata ti reca.**

*The one wishing you evil will bring you bad news.*

**L'ambizione, l'odio e la vendetta muoiono sempre di fame.**

*Ambition, hatred and vengeance always starve to death.*

*Because the three of them are insatiable.*

**Dagli amici mi guardi Iddio, che dai nemici mi guardo io.**

*May God protect me from my friends and may I protect myself from my enemies.*

*It is harder to protect yourself from a person you trust who is fallacious, than to keep a foe away.*

**D'amore si muore e di odio si vive.**

*One dies from love and lives from hate.*

**Le armi portano pace.**

*Weapons bring peace.*

*Understand by dissuasion or after chaos, peace finally returns.*

**Chi invidia crepa.**

*The one who envies, dies.*

**L'ira turba la mente e acceca la ragione.**

Hatred troubles the spirit and blinds reasoning.

**Amor non ha ragione, ira non ha consiglio.**

Love has no reason, hate has no advice.

**La fine dell'ira è il pentimento.**

The end of hate is repentance.

**Chi si abbandona all'ira prenota il rimorso.**

Who gives way to hatred, books remorse.

Hate will make the person do terrible things that he or she will then regret.

**Ira di fratelli, ira di diavoli.**

Brothers' hate, devils' hate.

**La rabbia è roba da cani.**

Hate is something for dogs.

***Chi per amor si piglia per rabbia si lascia.***

*Who gets married for love, will part for hate.*

***La rabbia avvelena il fegato.***

*Hate poisons the liver.*

***La rabbia o passa o ammazza.***

*Hate, either it goes or it kills.*

# XI. Envy        Invidia

**Nella maldicenza c'è sempre un po' di vero.**

*In slander, there is always a bit of truth.*

**La maldicenza è il piacere degli imbecilli.**

*Slander is the dumb people's pleasure.*

**La maldicenza è il veleno dell'amicizia.**

*Slander is the poison of friendship.*

**Molti son più per la maldicenza che per la lode.**

*Many say more slander than praise.*

**Per vivere bisogna imparare a sopportare la maldicenza.**

*To live, we have to learn to bear slander.*

***L'invidia se stessa lacera.***

*Envy lacerates itself.*
*Someone destroys oneself with hate and envy.*

***L'invidioso è il carnefice di se stesso.***

*The envious is an executioner for himself.*

***L'invidia muore con l'invidioso.***

*Envy dies with the envious.*

*In the way that it can last for a life time.*

***Né fiamma senza fumo, né virtù senza invidia.***

*No smoke without fire and no talent without envy.*

***L'invidia cresce su ogni terreno.***

*Envy grows in every soil.*

***D'invidia si vive.***

*From envy, one can live.*

*Envy can be so immense to obsess someone and pace one's life.*

**Chi invidia crepa.**

*Who envies, dies from it.*

**L'invidioso si rode e l'invidiato gode.**

*The envious gnaws him, the envied is pleased.*

**Pane invidiato, con gusto mangiato.**

*The envied bread has more flavors.*

**L'invidiato mangia pane e l'invidioso muore di fame.**

*The envied person eats bread and the envious starves to death.*

**Muoiono gli invidiosi ma non l'invidia.**

*The envious dies but envy stays.*

**Chi non ebbe invidiosi non ebbe fortuna.**

*Who is not envied has no fortune.*

**Non fu gloria senza invidia.**

*There has never been glory without envy.*

**In Paradiso non si va in carozza.**

*No one will go to Heaven with a carriage.*

# XII. Legality
## Legalità

**Fidarsi è bene, non fidarsi è meglio.**

Trust is good, mistrust is better.

**Aceto rubato è più dolce del latte comprato.**

Stolen vinegar is sweeter than purchased milk.

**La prima arte è quella d'arrangiarsi.**

The first art is (to know how) to come to an agreement (with someone).

**Per arricchire basta voltar le spalle al Cristo.**

To become rich, you just need to turn your back to the Christ.

**In casa di ladri non si ruba.**

*In the house of thieves, one should not steal.*

**Nessun ladro è ladro finché non è scoperto.**

*No thief is a thief until he is discovered.*

**Il ladro è un mestiere che rende, ma è pericoloso.**

*Stealing is a job that pays, but it is dangerous.*

**La legge è legge.**

*Law is law.*

*Law is equal for all.*

**Ogni paese ha la sua legge.**

*Each village has its own law.*

*Understand rules and customs*

**La legge è per i poveri e per i coglioni.**

*Law is for poor people and idiots.*

*Legge e giustizia son due cose diverse.*

Law and justice are two different things.

*Dal lavoro onesto non viene la ricchezza.*

From honest work, one will not become wealthy.

*Molte leggi, poca obbedienza.*

Many laws and little obedience.

*Il potere è nella canna del fucile.*

Power is in the riffle.

*A rubar poco si va in galera.*
*A rubar molto si fa carriera.*

If one steals little, one will go to jail.
If one steals a lot, one will make a career.

*Bisogna rubare tanto o nulla.*

One should either steal a lot or nothing.

**Chi ruba allo Stato fa poco peccato.**

Who steals to the State does not commit a big sin.

**Rubare al Re, peccato non è.**

Stealing from the King is not a sin.

**Rubare ai ladri non è peccato.**

Stealing from thieves is not a sin.

**Nessuno è senza colpa.**

No one is without guilt.

**Peccato, grosso o niente.**

Sin, either big or nothing.

**Son più i peccatori dei Santi.**

There are more sinners than Saints.

**Una mano lava l'altra.**

One hand washes the other.

**A ogni uccello il suo nido è bello.**

*Every bird finds its nest beautiful.*

# XIII. Freedom — Libertà

**Pesce fuggito non canta in padella.**

Fish to flight will not sing in the pan.

**Nessun albero ne vuole un'altro sopra.**

No tree wants another above it.

No one will bear harsh competition.

**L'aquila vola sempre sola.**

The eagle always flies alone.

**Meglio un'oncia di libertà che dieci libbre d'oro.**

Better one ounce of freedom than ten pounds of gold.

**La libertà non si vende al mercato.**

*Freedom is not sold on the market place.*

*Therefore it is priceless.*

**Meglio libero e povero, che schiavo con le catene d'oro.**

*Better free and poor than a slave with golden chains.*

**Chi è libero non sa quanto è fortunato.**

*Who is free does not know one's fortune.*

**Ognuno è libero di fare quello che vuole.**

*Everyone is free to do what one wants.*

**La pecora libera finisce in bocca al lupo.**

*The free goat ends up in the wolf's mouth.*

**La libertà non c'è oro che la paghi.**

*Freedom is priceless.*

*Literally: Freedom, there is no gold to pay for it.*

**La libertà costa come la vita.**

*Freedom is as valuable as life.*

**Chi di libertà è privo, ha in odio d'esser vivo.**

*Someone deprived of freedom, hates to be alive.*

**Libertà e sanità valgon più di una città.**

*Freedom and health are worth more than a city.*

**La libertà del povero è mendicare in pace.**

*The poor man's freedom is to beg in peace.*

# XIV. Ill will — Malavoglia

**Le parole volano, gli scritti restano.**

Words fly away and written (documents) remain.

**Dal dire al fare c'è di mezzo il mare.**

Between saying and doing, there is the sea.

Easier said than done.

**Molto fumo e niente arrosto.**

A lot of smoke and no roasted meat.

Only small talks and no actions.

**Mal si caccia col cane che abbaia.**

One hunts badly with a dog that barks.
It is hard to come to an agreement with someone talking too much and promising a lot without maintaining.

***Chi abusa poco usa.***

*Who abuses, uses little.*

*Excess in every field is negative.*

***A chi non vuole aiutare, non mancano le scuse.***

*The one not wanting to help will always have excuses.*

***Altro è promettere, altro è mantenere.***

*One thing is to promise, another to maintain (what one has promised).*

***Il pesce si prende coll'amo e l'uomo con la parola.***

*The fish is caught with a hook, man is caught with words.*

***Ognuno pensa all'anima sua.***

*Everyone thinks of one's soul.*

**Lamentarsi, grattarsi e bere acqua non costa nulla.**

To complain, to scratch yourself and to drink water don't cost anything.

**Nessuno pecca controvoglia.**

Nobody sins against one's will.

There is no such thing as: "I didn't want to do it…"

**La pancia non si riempie di belle parole.**

Someone cannot fill his own belly with pretty words.

**Chi non ha parola non ha onore.**

Someone that has no word has no honor.

**Chi vuol fare fatti non dica parole.**

Someone who wants to act does not say a word.

**Le parole convincono, gli esempi spingono.**

The words convince and the examples attest.

**Chi troppo dice niente fa.**

Who speaks too much does not do a thing.

**Molte parole, pochi fatti.**

A lot of words and not many facts (understand actions).

**Le buone parole non costano nulla.**

Nice words are free.

**Il gallo canta bene e razzola male.**

The rooster sings well but scratches badly.

The one always teaching lessons and morals, always giving tips, usually does not follow what he preaches.

***Il gallo canta con gli occhi chiusi per far vedere che la sa a memoria.***

*The rooster sings with its eyes closed to show that it knows the song by heart.*

*For someone pretending to be an intellectual.*

# Risk — Rischio

**Spendere e spandere.**

Spend and spread.

To take financial risks without keeping a refuge.

**Chi lascia la strada vecchia per la nuova sa quel che lascia ma non sa quel che trova.**

Someone leaving the old way (road) for a new one knows which one he leaves behind but does not know which one he will find.

**Uomo avvisato mezzo salvato.**

An advised man is half way saved.

**L'agnello più vispo è quello che il lupo mangia per primo.**

It is the most daring lamb that the wolf eats first.

***Chi taglia l'albero perde i frutti e l'ombra.***

*Who cuts the tree loses the fruits and the shade.*

***Grande altezza, grande pericolo.***

*Big height, big danger.*

*The one taking big risks can all of a sudden lose everything.*

***Chi sale in alto diventa un bersaglio.***

*Who distinguishes oneself will become a target.*

*The more someone becomes powerful, the more envy and jealousy he or she will have to face.*

***Chi vuole il dolci non rifiuti l'amaro.***

*Someone wanting the sweet will not refuse the bitter.*

*There is always a drawback to everything, even glory and wealth.*

***Meglio perdere l'anello che il dito.***

*Better lose the ring than the finger.*

**Chi entra in mare e non sa nuotare, corre il rischio d'annegare.**

*Who enters in the sea and does not know how to swim, risks to drawn.*

**Chi teme l'ape non lecca il miele.**

*Who fears the bee will not lick the honey.*

**Chi non rischia non arricchisce.**

*Who does not take risks will not become wealthy.*

**Quando non si può, non si deve.**

*When it is no allowed, you should not.*

*Even if you have the opportunity to do something illegal, the consequences are too big.*

**E' re chi ruba un regno
Ladro chi ruba un legno.**

*The one stealing a kingdom is a king.
The one stealing wood is a thief.*

**Chi ruba una spilla in prigione
Chi ruba una villa è barone.**

*The one stealing a needle goes to jail.
The one stealing a villa becomes a Baron.*

**Pane rubato sveglia l'appetito.**

*Stolen bread awakes the appetite.*

**Rubare si può, ma non farsi prendere.**

*One can steal but should not be caught.*

**Il peccato arriva ridendo e se ne va piangendo.**

*The sin arrives laughing and leaves crying.*

*An illegal opportunity may seem interesting at first, but the consequences are heavy and the person will look back with bitterness.*

**Meglio perdere un occhio che la testa.**

*Better lose one's eye than one's head.*

**Non ti mettere con chi non ha nulla da perdere.**

*Don't go with someone who has nothing to lose.*

**Assai vince chi non gioca.**

*Someone not gambling will win a lot.*

*Starting by the savings he or she will make not losing money.*

**Chi nulla rischia nulla ottiene.**

*Who does not risk, does not gain.*

**Chi troppo rischia tutto perde.**

*Who takes big risks loses everything.*

# XV. Health — Salute

**Chi va piano va sano...e va lontano.**

Who goes slowly, goes surely... and goes far.

One should take the time to do things well without rushing and without forcing his or her physical capacities.
In a dialog, this expression is often started by one and ended by the other person.

**Dove entra il sole non entra il medico.**

Where the sun goes, the doctor doesn't go.

**Con l'acqua non ci si ammala, non ci si ubriaca e non ci s'indebita.**

With water, one doesn't get sick, doesn't get drunk, and doesn't run into debt.

**L'allegria è d'ogni male il rimedio universale.**

*Happiness in the universal remedy.*

**Allegria fa bel viso.**

*Happiness makes a pretty face.*

**Finché si è allegri, non si muore.**

*As long as one is happy, one will not die.*

**Alzarsi presto e andare a letto presto fanno l'uomo sano e ricco.**

*Get up and go to bed early make the healthy and rich man.*

**Credere di essere malato è l'inizio della guarigione.**

*To acknowledge being sick is the beginning of healing.*

**I sani fanno di tutto per ammalarsi
E i malati fan di tutto per guarire.**

*Healthy people do everything they can to get sick and sick people do everything they can to heal.*

**L'ammalato chiede a Dio una cosa e il sano molto.**

*The sick person asks only one thing to God, whereas the healthy person asks many things.*

**Se il medico non può salvare il corpo, il prete salverà l'anima.**

*If the doctor cannot save the body, the priest will save the soul.*

**Quando c'è la salute, c'è tutto.**

*When health is there, there is everything.*

**La salute vale più della richezza.**

*Health is worth more than wealth.*

**Non c'è denaro che possa pagare la salute.**

*No money can buy health.*

**Il bene della salute si conosce quando si perde.**

One realizes the value of being healthy when one gets sick.

**La sanità vale più che un castello.**

Health is worth more than a castle.

**La salute è la figlia della temperanza.**

Health is the daughter of temperance.

**La temperanza è la guardiana della vita.**

Temperance is life's guardian.

**La temperanza ti fa signore.**

Temperance makes a lord out of you.

# XVI. Society        Società

**Tutto il mondo è paese.**

The world is a village.


**Il paese dove il "sí" suona.**

The country where the « Sí » sounds.

To describe Italy, the "Belpaese", the "beautiful country". Note this expression underlines Italian people's joy of life and exuberance.


**Chi va con lo zoppo, impara a zoppicare.**

One learns to limp with the lame man.

Someone will always be influenced by one's environment and circle of friends.


**Andate a farvi benedire!**

Go to get blessed!

***Va a farti friggere!***

*Go to get fried!*


***Bacco, tabacco e Venere riducon l'uomo in cenere.***

*Bacchus (The God of wine for Romans), tobacco and Venus will reduce a man to dust.*


***Paese che vai, usanze che trovi.***

*Country you go to, (other) customs you will find.*

*Customs vary in every country in the world. No one will ever adapt to the foreigner, but the foreigner will have to respect and follow the use and customs.*


***Ovunque vai, fa come vedrai.***

*Where ever you go, do as you will see.*

*Respect and follow local customs.*


***Partire è un po' morire.***

*To leave is a little bit like dying.*

*This expression is used for a trip as well as for Italians that left home and migrated to another country.*

**Tutte le strade conducono a Roma.**

*All the roads lead to Rome.*

**L'albergo della luna.**

The moon hotel.
To sleep in the open.

**Nessuna nuova, buona nuova.**

No news, good news.

**A cavallo donato, non si guarda in bocca.**

One should not examine the mouth of the horse one receives as a grant.

Don't be squeamish about something you receive for free or as a gift.

**Chi la vuol allesso e chi arrosto.**

Some like it boiled and others roasted.

Opinions are often if not always different.

**Il figlio del calzolaio ha le scarpe rotte.**

The shoe mender's son has broken shoes.

**Fare il pelo e il contropelo.**

To rub someone up the wrong way.

**Meglio voltarsi a Dio che ai Santi.**

Better devote yourself to God than to His Saints.

**Pezzo da museo**

Museum piece.

Expression used to describe an "old bat".

**Casa mia, casa mia, per piccina che tu sia, tu mi sembri una badia.**

*My home, my home, even though you are small, you seem like an abbey to me.*

**E' sempre la stessa musica.**

*It is always the same music.*

**Tutti siamo figli di Adamo e di Eva.**

*We are all children of Adam and Eve.*

**Siamo tutti fatti di una pasta.**

*We are all made of the same stuff.*

*"Pasta" means dough, paste and pasta! But of course let's not play with words.*

**Talvota vale l'ago, dove non vale la spada.**

*Sometimes the needle wins where the sword has lost.*

*Violence and strength does not always pay, especially giving advice. Some kind words and explanations can be much more effective.*

*L'amore è bello quando comincia,*
*Il prosciutto quando è a metà*
*E la predica quando finisce.*

*Love is beautiful when it starts,*
*Ham is (good) when it is half eaten,*
*And the Sermon, when it is over.*


*L'amore è per chi sogna,*
*La fortuna è per chi dorme,*
*La ragione è per chi veglia*
*E il perdono è per chi muore.*

*Love is for the one who dreams,*
*Luck, for the one who sleeps,*
*Reason, for the one who stays up,*
*And forgiveness, for the one who dies.*


**Anima non giudica anima**

*A soul cannot judge another soul.*

*Only God can judge.*


**Sanno molto più gli anni che i libri.**

*Books know more than years.*
*Education brings more than experience.*

*Tra il parere e l'essere*
*Ci sta quanto tra il cucire e il tessere.*

*In between appearing and being,*
*There is as much difference as between sewing and weaving.*

*Never judge a book by its cover.*

*Lamentarsi è un vizio.*

*To complain is a vice.*

*L'invidia adora la mediocrità.*

*Envy loves mediocrity.*

*Chi più può più fa.*

*Who can do more, does more.*

*The possibilities are greater for the ones who can financially assume them.*

*Ognuno ruba per conto suo.*

*Everyone steals for himself.*

**Chi non ruba non vince.**

Who does not steal, doesn't make it.

**Il popolo è il peggior tiranno.**

The people are the worst tyrants.

**Una voce non fa il popolo.**

One voice does not make the people's voice.

**Il popolo fa come l'asino che porta il vino e che beve acqua.**

The people do as the donkey that carries the wine and drinks the water.

**I popoli si ammazzano e i re si abbracciano.**

The people kill one another and the kings embrace.

**Molto bene lo fa chi non fa male.**

*The one who did not harm, already did a lot of good.*

*It is easy to hurt someone's feelings, especially giving some advice.*

**Anche nel brutto non si deve esagerare.**

*Even in evil, no one should exaggerate.*

**Fai del bene ai pezzenti e in capo a un anno ti cavano gli occhi.**

*Do some good to ungrateful people and after a year, they will put out your eyes.*

# XVII. Weather, Time
## Tempo

**Sotto la neve, il pane.**

Under snow, bread.

*The best years for agriculture are often the coldest ones.*

**Dopo il fulmine, il sereno.**

*After the storm, the good weather.*

**L'età porta senno.**

*Age brings wisdom.*

**La sola ricchezza insostituibile è il tempo.**

*The only irreplaceable wealth is time.*

***Meglio tardi che mai.***

*Better late than never.*

***Se gioventú sapesse, se vecchiaia potesse.***

*If the young knew, if the old could.*

*If the young had the experience of life...and the elderly, the strength and the energy.*

***La notte porta consiglio.***

*Night brings advice.*

*You have to sleep on every important decision, to allow a good time of reasoning.*

***Il mattino ha l'oro in bocca.***

*Morning has gold in the mouth.*

***Anno bisesto tutte le cose van di traverso.***

*During a bissextile year, everything goes wrong.*

***Acqua in strada, fiera in bottega.***

*Water in the street, fair in the stores.*
*Rainy days are good for shopping.*

**Anni e peccati, se ne dice sempre meno di quel che sono.**

*For years (age) and sins, people always say less than the truth.*

**Colla pioggia e col sole, sempre qualcuno è scontento.**

*With either rain or sunshine, there is always someone unhappy.*

**Il tempo è denaro.**

*Time is money.*

**Tutto vince il tempo.**

*Time wins on everything.*

**Il tempo tutto consuma.**

*Time consumes everything.*

**Chi tempo ha e tempo aspetta, tempo perde.**

Who has time and waits, loses time.

**Il tempo perso non è più di nessuno.**

Lost time does not belong to anybody anymore.

**Ogni frutto ha la sua stagione.**

Every season has its fruit.

**La bella stagione viene volando e la brutta nuotando.**

The beautiful season comes flying and the bad one comes swimming.

Summer comes with wind in March and autumn with rain.

**Chi non semina a primavera non raccoglie d'estate.**

Who does not sow in spring has no harvest in summer.

***D'estate ogni stronzo nuota.***

*In summer, all the idiots swim.*

*In summer, everything seems easier and therefore everyone takes a rest.*

***L'autunno spoglia le piante e veste gli uomini.***

*Autumn lays bare the plants and dresses men.*

# XVIII. Work/Art — Lavoro, Arte

**Il buon giorno si vede dal mattino.**

A good day can be seen from the morning.

**Impara l'arte e mettila da parte.**

Learn the art (the mastership of a profession) and put it to the side.

**Facendo s'impara.**

We learn as we make.

**Acquista fama e dormi**

Acquire fame and sleep.

Once reputation and fame are made, one can rest.

***Impara piangendo, riderai guagagnando.***
Learn crying and laugh earning.

***Volere è potere***

To want is to be able to.

When there is good will, there is a way.

***Navigare è necessario, non è necessario vivere.***

To navigate is necessary, it is not necessary to live.

Italy is very linked to the sea and has many navy-men expressions.

***Avere il vento in poppa.***

To have the wind after.

To be favored by fortune.

***I viaggi formano la gioventú.***

Trips form youth.

*Traveling, young people learn a lot of things.*

**Meglio l'uovo oggi che la gallina domani.**

*Better the egg today than the hen tomorrow.*

*Beware of promises and excessive hope.*

**Vale più un asino vivo che un dottore morto.**

*A living donkey is worth more than a dead doctor.*

**La critica è facile, l'arte è difficile.**

*It is easy to criticize; it is hard to do art.*

*Easier said than done.*

**Contro la forza ragion non vale.**

*Against strength, reason doesn't count.*

**Aiutati, che Dio ti aiuta.**

*Help yourself so that God helps you.*

**Non si può fare di un asino uno scienziato.**

*We cannot make a scientist out of a donkey.*

**L'abitudine è una camicia di ferro.**

*A habit is an iron shirt.*

**Con la piccola accetta s'atterra un grosso albero.**

*With a little axe, one can cut down a big tree.*

**Negli affari non si conosce amico.**

*In business, don't recognize any friends.*

**Albero grande fa più ombra che frutta.**

*A big tree makes more shade than fruits.*

**L'albero che ha molti frutti non li mattura tutti.**

*The tree having many fruits will not grow them all ripe.*

*Tra amici, due testimoni e un notaio.*

In between friends (in business), two witnesses and a lawyer.

*Non c'è pane senza pena.*

There is no bread without pain.

No pain no gain.

*Sapere è potere.*

To know is to be able to.

Knowledge is power, in terms of education and culturally, with different customs.

*Il sapere non è mai troppo.*

Knowledge is never too much.

No one can say one learnt enough.

*Chi meno sa più crede di sapere.*

*The less someone knows, the more one thinks to know.*

**Si sa, dove siamo, ma non dove si va a finire.**

*We know where we are, not where we will end up.*

**Chi più sa meno crede.**

*The more one knows, the less one believes.*

**Il tuo nemico è quel dell'arte tua.**

*Your enemy is the one that makes the same art as you. (understand profession).*

**Se vuoi arricchire, fai un'arte vile.**

*If you want to get rich, make an evil job (understand a job no one wants to do).*

**Chi non sa l'arte chiuda la bottega.**

*Someone not knowing one's job is going out of business.*

**L'arte è lunga e la vita breve.**

*Learning how to master an art (profession) is long, but life is short.*

# XIX. Latin Proverbs – A Must

**Venni, vidi e vinsi**

I came, I saw, I won.

**Carpe diem**

Seize the day.

**Mens sana in corpore sano.**

In Italian,
Mente sano in corpo sano.

A healthy head in a healthy body.

**Melius est abundare quam deficere.**

Better be in abundance than to lack.

***Abyssus abyssum invocat.***

*The deep calls the deep.*

*In a vicious circle, a mistake many provoke a series of other mistakes and take the person always deeper.*

***Omnia vincit amor.***

*Love can conquer everything.*

***Invidia gloriae comes.***

*Envy is glory's mate.*

***Silent leges inter arma.***

*Weapons make law silent.*

***Sani divitibus ditiores.***

*The healthy people are richer than the rich.*

***Vox populi, vox Dei.***

*The people's voice is God's voice.*

**Nescit vox emissa reverti.**

*A word, once said, cannot be taken back.*

**Vox unius, vox nulius.**

*Voice of one, voice of no one.*

Made in the USA
San Bernardino, CA
01 August 2019